JAZZIN' A...
fun pieces for
PIANO/KEYBOARD DUET

CONTENTS

© 1996 by Faber Music Ltd
First published in 1996 by Faber Music Ltd
Bloomsbury House 74–77 Great Russell Street London WC1B 3DA
Music engraved by Chris Hinkins
Cover by velladesign
Printed in England by Caligraving Ltd
All rights reserved

ISBN10: 0-571-51662-9
EAN13: 978-0-571-51662-9

PAM WEDGWOOD
WITH SPECIAL THANKS TO FAY GREGORY

Big Mack

SECONDO

Big Mack

PRIMO

No return

SECONDO

No return

PRIMO

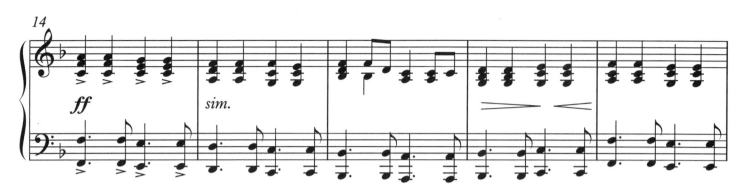

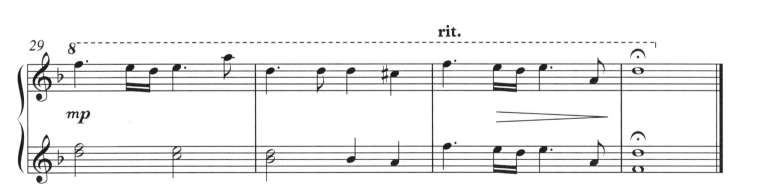

Amber

SECONDO

Amber

PRIMO

31

36

D.C. al ⊕ *poi al Coda*
poco rit.

40

CODA
poco rit.

43

Gold rush

SECONDO

Funky−lots of energy (♩ = c.112)

Gold rush

PRIMO

Finger bustin' Boogie

SECONDO

Finger bustin' Boogie

PRIMO

★ glissando – drag the finger or hand quickly down the white notes to the left hand note.

Enigma

SECONDO

Enigma

PRIMO

Steppe on it!

SECONDO

Steppe on it!

PRIMO

Tanglewood

SECONDO

Moderate swing tempo ($\quad$ = c.120)

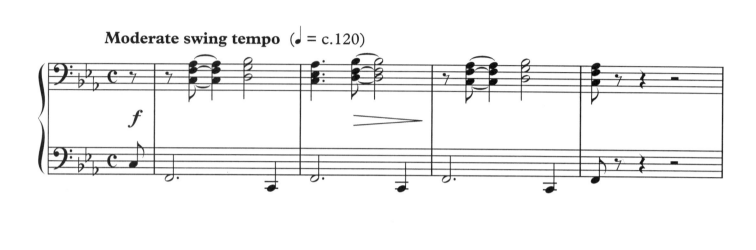

Tanglewood

PRIMO

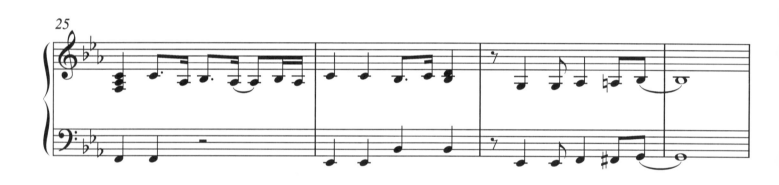

In the fast lane

SECONDO

In the fast lane

PRIMO

On the level

SECONDO

On the level

PRIMO

The JAZZIN' ABOUT series
PAM WEDGWOOD

Jazzin' About. Trumpet	ISBN 0-571-51039-6
Jazzin' About. Trombone	ISBN 0-571-56943-9
Jazzin' About. Alto Saxophone	ISBN 0-571-51054-X
Jazzin' About. Piano	ISBN 0-571-51105-8
Jazzin' About. Clarinet	ISBN 0-571-51273-9
Jazzin' About. Flute	ISBN 0-571-51275-5
Jazzin' About. Violin	ISBN 0-571-51315-8
Jazzin' About. Cello	ISBN 0-571-51316-6
Jazzin' About. Piano duet	ISBN 0-571-51662-9
Green Jazzin' About. Piano	ISBN 0-571-51645-9
Easy Jazzin' About. Piano	ISBN 0-571-51337-9
Easy Jazzin' About. Piano duet	ISBN 0-571-51661-0
Easy Jazzin' About. Descant Recorder	ISBN 0-571-52329-3
More Jazzin' About. Piano	ISBN 0-571-51437-5
Christmas Jazzin' About. Piano duet	ISBN 0-571-51584-3
Christmas Jazzin' About. Clarinet	ISBN 0-571-51585-1
Christmas Jazzin' About. Flute	ISBN 0-571-51586-X
Christmas Jazzin' About. Violin	ISBN 0-571-51694-7
Christmas Jazzin' About. Cello	ISBN 0-571-51695-5
Christmas Jazzin' About. Trumpet	ISBN 0-571-51696-3
Really Easy Jazzin' About. Piano	ISBN 0-571-52089-8
Really Easy Jazzin' About. Flute	ISBN 0-571-52097-9
Really Easy Jazzin' About. Clarinet	ISBN 0-571-52098-7
Really Easy Jazzin' About. Oboe	ISBN 0-571-52124-X
Really Easy Jazzin' About. Bassoon	ISBN 0-571-52138-X
Really Easy Jazzin' About. Trombone	ISBN 0-571-52139-8
Really Easy Jazzin' About. Horn	ISBN 0-571-52172-X
Really Easy Jazzin' About. Alto Saxophone	ISBN 0-571-52197-5
Really Easy Jazzin' About. Trumpet	ISBN 0-571-52198-3
Really Easy Jazzin' About. Violin	ISBN 0-571-52201-7
Really Easy Jazzin' About. Recorder	ISBN 0-571-52408-7
Really Easy Jazzin' About Studies. Piano	ISBN 0-571-52422-2
Jazzin' About. Piano (with CD)	ISBN 0-571-53400-7
More Jazzin' About. Piano (with CD)	ISBN 0-571-53401-5
Easy Jazzin' About. Piano (with CD)	ISBN 0-571-53402-3
Really Easy Jazzin' About. Piano (with CD)	ISBN 0-571-53403-1
Christmas Jazzin' About. Piano (with CD)	ISBN 0-571-53404-X
Jazzin' About Styles. Piano (with CD)	ISBN 0-571-53405-8
Jazzin' About Standards. Piano (with CD)	ISBN 0-571-53406-6
Easy Jazzin' About Standards. Piano (with CD)	ISBN 0-571-53407-4

To buy Faber Music publications or to find out about the full range of titles available
please contact your local music retailer or Faber Music sales enquiries:

Faber Music Ltd, Burnt Mill, Elizabeth Way, Harlow CM20 2HX
Tel: +44 (0) 1279 82 89 82   Fax: +44 (0) 1279 82 89 83
sales@fabermusic.com   fabermusic.com   expressprintmusic.com